iPhone 15: The Ultimate Guide to Apple's Dynamic Island Phone

Settings and Usage Handbook

by

McCray White

Table of Contents:

Introduction: Why the iPhone 15 is a game-changer for smartphone users

The iPhone 15 is the latest flagship device from Apple, and it offers a range of features that make it stand out from the competition. The iPhone 15 is not just an incremental upgrade from the previous models, but a revolutionary device that redefines what a smartphone can do. In this essay, I will discuss some of the top new features of the iPhone 15 and explain why they are game-changers for smartphone users.

One of the most noticeable features of the iPhone 15 is the Dynamic Island, which replaces the notch in the display. The Dynamic Island is a small circular area that houses the front-facing camera and other sensors, and it can change its shape and position depending on the context. For example, when watching a video or playing a game, the Dynamic Island can shrink or disappear to provide a full-screen experience. When using Face ID or taking a selfie, the Dynamic Island can expand or move to the center to capture the user's face. The Dynamic Island is a clever solution that maximizes the screen real estate and enhances the user interface.

Another feature that sets the iPhone 15 apart from other smartphones is the 48MP main camera, which is also available on the iPhone 15 Plus. The

48MP main camera uses a quad-pixel sensor that combines four pixels into one to produce high-quality images with low noise and high dynamic range. The 48MP main camera also supports super-high-resolution photos (24MP and 48MP), which can capture more details and allow for more editing options. The 48MP main camera is complemented by a 12MP ultra-wide camera and a 12MP telephoto camera, which offer a versatile zoom range and a wide field of view. The iPhone 15 also introduces new camera modes, such as Cinematic mode and Action mode, which enable users to create stunning videos with professional effects.

A third feature that makes the iPhone 15 a game-changer for smartphone users is the USB-C port, which replaces the Lightning port. The USB-C port is a universal connector that can be used for charging, data transfer, audio output, and video output. The USB-C port also supports fast charging and fast data transfer, which can save time and hassle for users. The USB-C port also opens up new possibilities for connecting the iPhone 15 to other devices and accessories, such as monitors, keyboards, mice, headphones, speakers, and more. The USB-C port is a welcome addition that simplifies and expands the connectivity options for the iPhone 15.

These are just some of the features that make the iPhone 15 a game-changer for smartphone users.

The iPhone 15 also boasts a faster A16 chip, a brighter and more colorful Super Retina XDR display, an improved battery life, and more. The iPhone 15 is not only a powerful and beautiful device, but also a smart and innovative one that offers a unique and satisfying user experience. The iPhone 15 is truly a device that changes the game for smartphone users.

Chapter 1: Getting Started with the iPhone 15

Welcome to the world of the iPhone 15, Apple's latest and most innovative smartphone. In this chapter, I will guide you through the exciting process of setting up your iPhone 15 and getting acquainted with its exceptional features. Prepare to embark on an extraordinary journey with your new device, as we explore everything from initial setup to customizing and utilizing its advanced capabilities.

1.1 How to Set Up Your iPhone 15

Before diving into the wonderful features of your new iPhone 15, it's essential to go through the setup process. Upon unboxing your device, you will be greeted by the sleek and stylish design that Apple is renowned for. The first step is to power on your device by pressing the side button. As the iPhone 15 boots up, a vibrant and vibrant display will illuminate, captivating your senses.

Next, you will be guided through a series of prompts to set up your device. Language selection, region settings, and Wi-Fi network connection are some of the initial steps you will encounter. Following that, you will have the option to restore your iPhone 15 from a previous backup or set it up as a new device. If you are upgrading from a previous iPhone or switching from an Android device, the restore option allows you to seamlessly transfer your data, apps, and settings to your new device, making the transition hassle-free.

Furthermore, you will be prompted to log in to your Apple ID or create a new one if you haven't already done so. Your Apple ID serves as your passport to the Apple ecosystem and unlocks numerous features, services, and personalized settings for your iPhone 15. Be sure to enter your Apple ID credentials accurately to ensure a smooth and secure login process.

Once you have completed the initial setup steps, your iPhone 15 will be ready to use. However, there are still a few essential settings you should go through to optimize your experience. These include enabling iCloud backup to safeguard your data, setting up a passcode or Face ID for enhanced security, and configuring your notification preferences.

Now that you have completed the setup process, you are ready to explore the endless possibilities that your iPhone 15 has to offer. From its powerful A-series chip to its remarkable camera capabilities and immersive display, this device is designed to enhance your digital lifestyle in ways you haven't imagined.

As you embark on your iPhone 15 journey, remember that this extraordinary device is packed with features and functionalities that will continue to amaze and inspire you. So seize the moment, embrace the possibilities, and let your iPhone 15 become your ultimate companion in the digital realm.

1.2 How to Use the Dynamic Island and Customize the Action Button

One of the standout features of the iPhone 15 is the introduction of the Dynamic Island and the versatile Action button. The Dynamic Island is a customizable area at the bottom of the iPhone 15's screen that adapts to your needs, providing quick access to frequently used apps and functions. The Action button, located within the Dynamic Island, allows for convenient and efficient navigation through various tasks.

To customize the Dynamic Island, simply tap and hold on any app icon or widget until the icons start jiggling. This indicates that you're in customization mode. From here, you can rearrange the placement of the app icons or widgets within the Dynamic Island by dragging them to your preferred positions. You can even add or remove items by tapping the "+" or "-" icons that appear during customization.

The Action button, situated within the Dynamic Island, offers a shortcut menu that provides immediate access to various functions and tasks. By default, the Action button displays commonly used options such as taking a quick photo, searching the web, or composing a new message. However, this button is fully customizable to suit your specific preferences.

To customize the Action button, tap and hold on it until a menu appears. Here, you can select the actions or shortcuts you want to be displayed within the Action button. Whether it's launching your favorite app, toggling settings like Wi-Fi or Bluetooth, or accessing your calendar for upcoming events, the Action button ensures effortless access to your most essential tasks.

By personalizing the Dynamic Island and Action button to align with your usage patterns, you can optimize the efficiency of your iPhone 15. This level of customization empowers you to have quick and convenient access to the apps and functions that matter most to you, saving valuable time and enhancing your overall iPhone experience.

1.3 How to Transfer Data from Your Old iPhone or Android Device

If you're upgrading from a previous iPhone or switching from an Android device, the iPhone 15 offers seamless data transfer to ensure a smooth transition. Apple provides the "Quick Start" feature, specifically designed to simplify the transfer process and ensure that all your essential data, including contacts, photos, apps, and settings, are carried over to your new device.

To transfer data from your old iPhone to your new iPhone 15, ensure that both devices are running on the latest version of iOS and are in close proximity. During the initial setup process, a prompt will appear on your new iPhone 15, offering to transfer data from your current device. Simply follow the on-screen instructions and authenticate the transfer using your Apple ID credentials or device passcode. The transfer will then commence, and you can monitor the progress on both devices.

If you're coming from an Android device, Apple provides the "Move to iOS" app, which simplifies the process of transferring your data. First, ensure that both devices are connected to a stable Wi-Fi network. On your iPhone 15, during the initial setup, select the "Move Data from Android" option and follow the prompts. Then, on your Android device, open the "Move to iOS" app and follow the instructions to establish a secure connection between the two devices. You can then select the data you want to transfer, such as contacts, messages, photos, and even your Google account information. The app will handle the transfer process seamlessly, ensuring your data is safely transferred to your new iPhone 15.

By utilizing the data transfer options available on the iPhone 15, you can seamlessly transition to your new device without the hassle of manually transferring data or settings. This ensures that you can continue using your new iPhone 15 with all your familiar content and settings intact, allowing for a smooth and uninterrupted user experience.

1.4 How to Use Face ID, Apple Pay, and Other Features

The iPhone 15 comes equipped with a range of advanced features, including Face ID and Apple Pay, that enhance security, convenience, and overall user experience. In this section, we will delve into these features, as well as highlight other notable functionalities of the iPhone 15.

Face ID, Apple's facial recognition technology, revolutionizes the way you unlock your iPhone 15 and authenticate various actions and transactions. Setting up Face ID is a clear process. Simply go to the Settings app on your iPhone, navigate to Face ID & Passcode, and set up your facial recognition by following the on-screen instructions. During setup, the iPhone 15 uses its TrueDepth camera system to scan and map your face, creating a detailed facial recognition profile unique to you. This sophisticated technology ensures a high level of accuracy and security when unlocking your device or authorizing secure transactions.

With Face ID enabled, all you need to do is look at your iPhone 15 to unlock it. The device will recognize your face and grant you access, saving you the inconvenience of using a password or Touch ID. Additionally, Face ID supports various features such as seamless app authentication, secure access to private information within apps, and effortless transactions with Apple Pay.

Apple Pay offers a simple, secure, and convenient way to make payments using your iPhone 15. With Face ID, Apple Pay transactions become even more streamlined and secure. When making a payment in a store or within apps, simply authenticate using Face ID by looking at your iPhone 15, and the payment will be authorized. This eliminates the need for physical cards or entering your payment details manually, ensuring a seamless and secure payment experience.

Beyond Face ID and Apple Pay, the iPhone 15 boasts a myriad of other notable features. These include an impressive camera system that allows you to capture stunning photos and videos, including immersive cinematic experiences with the enhanced Dolby Vision HDR recording capabilities. The device also supports advanced augmented reality (AR) functionality, enabling you to experience immersive AR apps and games that blend the virtual and real world seamlessly.

The iPhone 15 also maintains Apple's commitment to privacy and security. It incorporates advanced encryption techniques to safeguard your personal data and offers a comprehensive set of privacy controls, empowering you to have full control over your digital privacy. With features like App Tracking Transparency, you can choose which apps can track your data across other apps or websites.

Furthermore, the iPhone 15 consistently receives software updates that introduce new features, enhancements, and security improvements. These updates not only ensure your device remains up to date but also introduce exciting functionalities and strengthen the overall performance of your iPhone 15.

By utilizing the power of Face ID, the convenience of Apple Pay, and exploring the extensive array of features offered by the iPhone 15, you can fully optimize your experience and leverage the full potential of your device. The combination of these features ensures enhanced security, seamless transactions, and unparalleled convenience, enabling you to make the most of your iPhone 15 and enjoy a truly captivating digital experience.

I hope this detailed explanation helps you understand how to use Face ID, Apple Pay, and other notable features of the iPhone 15. Let's move on to the next chapter!

Chapter 2: Exploring the iPhone 15's Display and Camera

Get ready to be captivated by the immersive experience offered by the iPhone 15's remarkable display and camera capabilities. In this chapter, we will delve into the stunning Super Retina XDR display and HDR video, as well as explore the advanced photography and videography features of the 48MP Main camera, Ultra Wide lens, and Telephoto lens. Prepare to unleash your creativity and capture unforgettable moments with unparalleled clarity and brilliance.

2.1 How to Enjoy the Super Retina XDR Display and HDR Video

The iPhone 15 boasts the Super Retina XDR display, which takes viewing quality to new heights. With its vibrant colors, deep blacks, and remarkable brightness, this display ensures an immersive visual experience. Whether you're streaming movies, playing games, or browsing your photo collection, every detail comes to life on the iPhone 15's screen.

Furthermore, the iPhone 15 supports HDR video playback, which enhances the dynamic range and color accuracy of supported content. HDR (High Dynamic Range) videos offer a broader spectrum of colors and highlights and shadows that are more true to life. When viewing HDR content on your iPhone 15, you'll witness a new level of realism and visual depth, especially in scenes with extreme brightness or darkness.

To fully enjoy the Super Retina XDR display and HDR video capabilities, make sure to explore the vast range of HDR content available on various streaming platforms. Whether you're watching movies, TV shows, or videos shot in HDR, you'll appreciate the remarkable clarity, contrast, and color representation that bring the content to life.

Adjusting display settings on your iPhone 15 allows you to further optimize your viewing experience. Under Display & Brightness settings, you can adjust the brightness level, enable True Tone for accurate color representation in different lighting conditions, and adjust accessibility features such as text size and font styling.

Immerse yourself in breathtaking visuals, vibrant colors, and exceptional contrast with the Super Retina XDR display, and enhance your viewing experience with the magic of HDR video on your iPhone 15.

2.2 How to Take Stunning Photos and Videos with the 48MP Main Camera and the Ultra Wide and Telephoto Lenses

The iPhone 15 is equipped with a powerful camera system, allowing you to capture stunning photos and videos with professional-level quality. It features a 48MP Main camera, Ultra Wide lens, and Telephoto lens that combine to offer unparalleled versatility and creative possibilities.

The 48MP Main camera serves as the primary lens, providing exceptional clarity and detail in every shot. Whether you're capturing landscapes, portraits, or close-up shots, this camera ensures extraordinary image quality. The high resolution allows for ample room for cropping or zooming in on your photos without compromising quality.

The Ultra Wide lens expands your creative horizons by allowing you to capture vast landscapes, group shots, and immersive cityscapes. With its wider field of view, you can fit more into the frame and create breathtaking compositions that showcase the entirety of a scene. This lens adds depth and perspective to your photos, making them more dynamic and engaging.

For those moments when you need to get closer to your subject, the Telephoto lens comes into play. It offers a closer zoom capability, enabling you to capture incredible detail even from a distance. Whether it's photographing wildlife, sporting events, or capturing candid moments, the Telephoto lens ensures sharp focus and beautiful bokeh effects for stunning portraits.

In addition to the lenses themselves, the iPhone 15's camera system is further enhanced by advanced features that elevate your photography experience. It incorporates features such as Smart HDR, which intelligently analyzes the scene to capture a broader dynamic range and preserve details in highlights and shadows. Night mode allows for impressive low-light photography, capturing clear and vibrant images even in dimly lit environments.

2.3 How to Use Cinematic Mode, Action Mode, Photographic Styles, and Other Camera Modes

The iPhone 15 introduces exciting camera modes and features that let you unleash your creativity and capture extraordinary moments. Among these is Cinematic mode, which enables you to shoot videos with a stunning depth-of-field effect, typically associated with professional cinematography. It adds a beautiful bokeh background blur to your videos, keeping the main subject in sharp focus while creating a cinematic ambiance.

Action mode is designed to capture fast-paced and dynamic moments in crisp detail. It utilizes advanced image stabilization and focus tracking, allowing you to freeze action sequences or capture moving subjects with remarkable clarity. Whether you're photographing sports, pets, or any other fast-moving subjects, Action mode ensures you never miss a moment.

Photographic Styles is a feature that allows you to customize the tone and look of your photos. It offers a range of presets tailored to different aesthetics such as vibrant, rich contrast, or muted tones. By experimenting with Photographic Styles, you can further personalize your photos and achieve the desired mood you envision for your images.

Beyond these specific modes, the iPhone 15 offers a variety of other camera capabilities to enhance your photography experience. From Time-lapse to Panorama, Slo-mo to Portrait mode, each mode presents unique opportunities to explore different styles and techniques.

With the iPhone 15's powerful camera system and an array of exciting modes and features, you can unleash your creativity and capture stunning photos and videos like never before. Whether it's seizing breathtaking landscapes, documenting special moments, or exploring artistic expressions, the iPhone 15 empowers you to capture unforgettable memories with professional-level quality.

2.4 How to Edit and Share Your Photos and Videos with Photos, iMovie, and Other Apps

Capturing stunning photos and videos is just the beginning. With the iPhone 15, you have a multitude of options to edit and enhance your visual creations, allowing you to refine your images and videos to perfection. In this section, we will explore the powerful editing tools and options available to you through the built-in Photos app, iMovie, and other third-party apps.

The Photos app on your iPhone 15 offers a range of editing capabilities that enable you to enhance your photos effortlessly. From basic adjustments to advanced edits, you have the tools to refine your images. With a simple tap, you can crop, straighten, or apply automatic adjustments that enhance exposure, color balance, and overall image quality. Additionally, you can manually adjust parameters such as brightness, contrast, saturation, and more to achieve the desired look for your photos.

Furthermore, the Photos app provides access to advanced editing tools like Curves, Selective Color, and Noise Reduction, allowing you to fine-tune your images with precision. These tools offer greater control over specific aspects of your photos, empowering you to create truly striking visuals. Experiment with different edits and adjustments to add your artistic touch and bring out the best in your photos.

When it comes to video editing, iMovie is a powerful tool that comes preinstalled on your iPhone 15. It offers a comprehensive suite of video editing features, allowing you to create professional-looking videos with ease. With iMovie, you can trim, crop, and combine clips, add transitions, apply filters, and incorporate titles and music to bring your videos to life. The intuitive interface and user-friendly controls make it accessible to both beginners and more experienced editors.

For those seeking additional editing capabilities, numerous third-party apps are available on the App Store. Apps like Adobe Lightroom, VSCO, or LumaFusion offer advanced editing features and allow you to fine-tune your photos or videos even further. They provide a wide range of creative adjustment options, filters, and effects to add your unique style and flair.

Once you're satisfied with your edited photos or videos, sharing them with family, friends, or the world is seamless on your iPhone 15. The Photos app allows you to easily share your creations directly from the app through various channels like Messages, Mail, or social media platforms. You can also create albums, slideshows, or shared albums to curate and present your best work.

When it comes to video sharing, iMovie and other video editing apps provide options to export your edited videos to various platforms or share them directly on social media. Whether it's creating a cinematic masterpiece or a fun vlog, these apps enable you to deliver your videos to your desired audience with ease.

By utilizing the editing tools available through the built-in Photos app, iMovie, and third-party apps, you can transform your still photos and videos into stunning visual storytelling. Experiment with different effects, styles, and adjustments to achieve your desired look and share your artistry with the world.

Remember, the editing process is an opportunity to express your creativity and take your visual creations to the next level. Enjoy the journey of refining your photos and videos, and let your imagination and artistic vision guide you.

I hope this detailed explanation helps you understand how to edit and share your photos and videos using the built-in Photos app, iMovie, and other apps on your iPhone 15. Let's move on to the next chapter!

Chapter 3: Boosting your productivity and creativity with the iPhone 15

In today's fast-paced world, where time is of the essence, it's important to find ways to enhance our productivity and maximize our creativity. With the cutting-edge features of the iPhone 15, you have a powerful tool at your fingertips that can help you achieve these goals. In this chapter, we will explore various ways to make the most of your iPhone 15 and leverage its capabilities to boost your productivity and unleash your creativity..

3.1 How to use Siri, Shortcuts, Widgets, and other tools to automate tasks and save time

Efficiency is the key to productivity, and the iPhone 15 offers several features that help you automate tasks and save precious time. Siri, Apple's intelligent personal assistant, can be your reliable companion in accomplishing various tasks with just a voice command. Whether you want to set reminders, make appointments, send messages, or even control your smart home devices, Siri is there to assist you.

To fully leverage Siri, take the time to customize its settings and train it to recognize your voice accurately. By enabling "Hey Siri," you can summon the assistant hands-free, allowing for a seamless workflow. Siri can also be integrated with other apps and services, such as third-party messaging apps, ride-sharing platforms, and even food delivery services, making your life even easier.

Furthermore, the iPhone 15 introduces Shortcuts, a powerful automation tool that enables you to create custom shortcuts for various tasks. From simple actions like sending pre-defined messages to complex workflows that involve multiple apps, Shortcuts empowers you to streamline your daily routine. Take advantage of the extensive Shortcuts library provided by Apple or create your own personalized workflows for maximum efficiency.

Widgets are another indispensable feature of the iPhone 15 that allows you to access pertinent information and perform quick actions right from your home screen. Organize your widgets according to your preferences, pinning the ones you use most frequently or those that provide time-sensitive information. By customizing your widgets, you can get a glimpse of your calendar events, weather updates, news headlines, and much more at a glance, without even opening the respective apps.

In addition to Siri, Shortcuts, and Widgets, the iPhone 15 also offers other tools to help automate tasks and save time. The powerful automation capabilities extend throughout the operating system, allowing you to create automations based on certain triggers or conditions. For instance, you can automate actions like turning on Do Not Disturb mode during meetings or adjusting screen brightness based on your location.

With these tools at your disposal, you can significantly reduce manual effort and spend more time on the tasks that truly require your attention. By automating repetitive tasks and mundane workflows, you can free up your energy and creativity for more meaningful endeavors.

3.2: How to use Notes, Reminders, Calendar, Mail, and other apps to organize your work and life

In today's fast-paced world, staying organized is crucial to maximizing productivity and effectively managing both your personal and professional life. The iPhone 15 offers a range of powerful apps that can assist you in achieving this goal. In this chapter, we will explore how to use Notes, Reminders, Calendar, Mail, and other apps to enhance your organizational skills and streamline your daily routine.

Notes: Capturing and organizing information seamlessly

The Notes app on the iPhone 15 is a versatile tool that allows you to jot down ideas, create checklists, and even draw sketches. It enables you to capture and organize information effortlessly, so you never miss a crucial detail. With the latest updates, the Notes app has become even more powerful, offering enhanced collaboration features and integrations.

To make the most of the Notes app, it is important to understand its key features and how to effectively utilize them:

- **Text Formatting**: Use various formatting options such as headers, bullet points, and bold/italic text to structure your notes and make them more readable.

- **Checklists**: Create to-do lists by adding checkboxes to your notes, enabling you to keep track of your tasks and mark them as completed once done.

- **Sketches and Photos**: The drawing tool in Notes allows you to sketch diagrams or take handwritten notes using either your finger or an Apple Pencil. Additionally, you can add photos from your camera roll or capture images directly within the app.

- **Organizing Notes**: Tagging your notes with relevant keywords and grouping them into folders or categories makes it easier to locate and access them in the future. You can also search for specific notes using the built-in search functionality.
- **Collaboration**: Share your notes with others to collaborate on projects or brainstorm ideas

together. Notes now enables real-time collaboration, allowing multiple users to edit and view the note simultaneously.

By leveraging these features, you can transform the Notes app into a powerful tool for managing your personal and professional information effectively.

Reminders: Staying on top of your tasks and commitments

The Reminders app on the iPhone 15 helps you stay organized by providing a platform to manage your tasks and commitments. Whether it's a simple grocery list or a complex project with multiple subtasks, Reminders empowers you to create, prioritize, and complete your tasks efficiently.

Here are some tips to use the Reminders app effectively:

- Creating Lists and Tasks: Organize your tasks by creating different lists. For example, you can have separate lists for work, personal, or shopping-related tasks. Within each list, add individual tasks with due dates, reminders, and even subtasks.

- Siri Integration: Take advantage of Siri's voice commands to create and manage your reminders hands-free. Simply say, "Hey Siri, remind me to buy groceries tomorrow morning," and Siri will create a reminder with the specified details.

- Smart Suggestions: Reminders offers smart suggestions based on your usage patterns and the content of your messages. For instance, if someone mentions a dinner plan in a text message, Reminders might automatically suggest creating a reminder for it. These intelligent suggestions can save you time and ensure you don't overlook any commitments.

- Snooze and Priority: Prioritize your tasks by assigning deadlines, setting priorities, and snoozing reminders to a later time or date. This way, you can focus on the most important tasks without being overwhelmed by excessive notifications.

- Location-based Reminders: Take advantage of the iPhone's GPS capabilities to set location-based reminders. For example, you can create a reminder to pick up laundry when you leave the office. The app will trigger a notification when you reach the specified location.

By leveraging the features and capabilities of the Reminders app, you can optimize your task management and ensure you never miss important deadlines or commitments.

3.3 How to use Pages, Numbers, Keynote, GarageBand, and other apps to create

documents, spreadsheets, presentations, music, and more

The iPhone 15 comes equipped with a suite of powerful productivity apps, including Pages, Numbers, Keynote, and GarageBand. These apps allow you to create professional-quality documents, spreadsheets, presentations, music, and more from the convenience of your iPhone. In this section, we will explore how to make the most of these creative tools.

Pages: Crafting stunning documents on the go

Pages is Apple's word processing app that lets you create beautiful documents with ease. Whether you need to draft a letter, write a report, or design a brochure, Pages provides a comprehensive set of features to accomplish your tasks efficiently.

To maximize your productivity with Pages, consider the following tips:

- **Templates and Formatting**: - Templates and Formatting: Start with a professionally designed template or customize your document using various formatting tools provided by Pages, including fonts, styles, and colors. The app offers a wide range of templates for various needs, such as resumes, newsletters, and invitations.

- **Collaboration:** Share your documents with others to collaborate on projects. Pages allows real-time collaboration, enabling multiple users to simultaneously edit and view the document.

- **Media Integration:** Enhance your documents by seamlessly incorporating images, videos, and charts. You can easily insert multimedia elements from your Photos library or other online sources.

- **Export and Sharing**: Pages supports exporting your documents in multiple formats, including PDF, Word, and ePub. You can also share your documents directly from the app via email, Messages, or other popular communication platforms.

Numbers: Creating powerful spreadsheets effortlessly

Numbers is Apple's spreadsheet app that enables you to crunch numbers, visualize data, and analyze information efficiently. Whether it's financial reports, budget tracking, or data analysis, Numbers equips you with a rich array of features to handle complex calculations and presentation of data.

Here are some tips to make the most of Numbers:

- **Templates and Formulas**: Utilize pre-designed templates for common tasks like budgeting, invoices, and expense tracking. Additionally, take advantage of built-in functions and formulas to automate calculations and streamline your workflow.

- **Interactive Charts and Tables:** Present your data effectively by generating interactive charts and tables. Customize their appearance, apply different chart types, and explore visualizations to convey your findings accurately.

- **Collaboration**: Numbers' collaboration features allow you to work on spreadsheets simultaneously with others. Changes made by different users are synchronized in real-time, ensuring everyone stays updated.

- **Import and Export**: Import spreadsheets in various formats, including Microsoft Excel, CSV, and more. Similarly, export your spreadsheets in formats compatible with other software and platforms.

- **Data Analysis**: Leverage advanced features like sorting, filtering, and conditional formatting to analyze your data effectively. Numbers also offers the ability to generate charts based on data subsets, allowing you to identify trends and make data-driven decisions.

Keynote: Creating compelling presentations in minutes

Keynote is Apple's powerful presentation app that enables you to create visually stunning slideshows on your iPhone. Whether it's a pitch deck, lecture slides, or a creative portfolio, Keynote provides a wide range of tools to deliver captivating presentations.

To unleash the potential of Keynote, consider the following:

- Templates and Themes: Start with professionally designed templates or create your own unique design using various themes, fonts, and graphics options. Keynote offers a plethora of templates and styles, allowing you to tailor your presentation to the occasion.

- Transitions and Animations: Add engaging transitions and animationsto captivate your audience. Keynote provides intuitive tools to animate text, images, and shapes, giving your presentation a professional touch.

- Multimedia Integration: Enhance your slides by seamlessly incorporating images, videos, and audio recordings. Whether it's a captivating image or a video walkthrough of a product, Keynote lets you blend different media elements seamlessly.

- Presenter Tools: Keynote offers dedicated presenter tools that allow you to truly interact with your audience. You can use your iPhone as a remote control to advance slides, view notes, and even use your device as a teleprompter.

- **Export and Sharing**: Easily share your presentations with others via email, Messages, or other communication platforms. Keynote also supports exporting your slideshows in various formats, including PDF and PowerPoint.

GarageBand: Unleashing your musical creativity

GarageBand is an intuitive music creation app that transforms your iPhone into a portable music studio. Whether you're a beginner or an experienced musician, GarageBand offers a suite of powerful features to compose, record, and produce high-quality music.

To tap into your musical potential with GarageBand, consider the following tips:

- **Virtual Instruments**: GarageBand offers a wide range of virtual instruments, including keyboards, guitars, drums, and more. You can play these instruments using touch-sensitive controls or connect external MIDI keyboards for a more authentic experience.

- **Smart Instruments**: Use Smart Instruments to automatically produce chords, melodies, and beats, even if you have no prior music knowledge or skills. These intelligent tools allow you to create impressive compositions effortlessly.

- Recording and Mixing: GarageBand enables you to record audio tracks using built-in microphones or external audio interfaces. You can then edit the recorded tracks, apply effects, and mix them to achieve a polished sound.

- Loops and Samples: Access a vast collection of pre-recorded loops and samples to enhance your compositions. GarageBand offers loops for various genres, instruments, and moods, allowing you to create professional-sounding music in minutes.

- Sharing and Collaboration: Share your music with the world by exporting your tracks as audio files, ringtone files, or even directly to popular streaming platforms. Additionally, GarageBand supports collaboration, enabling you to work on music projects with other users remotely.

By harnessing the capabilities of Pages, Numbers, Keynote, and GarageBand on your iPhone 15, you can unleash your creativity in various domains and produce professional-grade results.

3.4 How to Use iCloud, AirDrop, AirPlay, and Other Services to Sync and Stream Your Data Across Devices

In today's interconnected world, the ability to seamlessly access and share your data across multiple devices is crucial. With the iPhone 15, Apple offers a range of services and features that allow you to sync and stream your data effortlessly. In this section, we will explore how to utilize iCloud, AirDrop, AirPlay, and other services to enhance your productivity and convenience.

iCloud is Apple's cloud storage and synchronization service, designed to keep your photos, videos, documents, contacts, and more up to date across all your devices. By enabling iCloud on your iPhone 15, you can effortlessly access your files from your iPad, Mac, or even the iCloud website. It ensures that your important data is securely stored and conveniently accessible wherever you go.

With iCloud Drive, you can store your files in the cloud and access them from any of your devices, providing a seamless experience as you switch between different devices. It also enables collaboration by allowing you to share files and folders with others, making it easy to work on projects together.

Another valuable feature of iCloud is iCloud Photos. By storing your photos and videos in iCloud, you can access them from any device and enjoy a consistent library of memories. Changes made to your photo library, such as edits or deletions, are synchronized across all devices, ensuring that your photo collection stays organized and up to date.

AirDrop is a powerful file-sharing feature that enables you to quickly and wirelessly transfer files between Apple devices. Whether you're sharing a photo, a document, or a video, AirDrop allows you to effortlessly send files to nearby devices with just a few taps. It's a convenient and secure way to share content without the need for cables or online file-sharing services.

AirPlay takes multimedia streaming to the next level. With AirPlay, you can wirelessly stream audio, video, and even mirror your iPhone 15's screen to an AirPlay-enabled device, such as an Apple TV or a smart TV. This enables you to enjoy your favorite movies, music, or presentations on a larger screen, enhancing your entertainment and productivity experiences.

In addition to these services, Apple provides a range of other synchronization features and services to streamline your digital life. These include Handoff, which allows you to seamlessly transition between devices while working on the same document, email, or browsing session. Continuity Camera lets you capture photos or scan documents directly from your iPhone 15 and have them instantly appear on your Mac. These features further enhance productivity and streamline workflows across your Apple devices.

By leveraging the power of iCloud, AirDrop, AirPlay, and other synchronization services, you can ensure that your data is accessible, up to date, and seamlessly shared across all your devices. This level of connectivity and synchronization empowers you to be productive, creative, and efficient, while experiencing a cohesive and connected digital ecosystem.

I hope this extensive explanation helps you understand how to use iCloud, AirDrop, AirPlay, and other services to sync and stream your data across devices with your iPhone 15. Let's move to the next chapter of this chapter.

Chapter 4: Having Fun and Staying Connected with the iPhone 15

The iPhone 15 offers a wide array of apps and features that allow you to have fun, stay connected, and enrich your digital lifestyle. In this chapter, we will explore how to utilize these apps to cmmunicate, browse the web, consume content, and access various services. Let's dive into the numerous possibilities offered by the iPhone 15.

4.1 How to Use Messages, FaceTime, Phone, and Other Apps to Communicate with Your Friends and Family

Communication is at the heart of the iPhone 15 experience, and Apple provides a range of apps to facilitate seamless communication with your friends and family.

The Messages app allows you to send text messages, photos, videos, and even personalized Animoji or Memoji to add flair to your conversations. You can engage in dynamic group conversations, react to messages with expressive emojis, and personalize your chats with customized effects and stickers.

FaceTime enables high-quality video and audio calls to connect with your loved ones, no matter where they are in the world. With the iPhone 15's advanced camera and audio capabilities, FaceTime calls feel incredibly lifelike and immersive. You can also take advantage of FaceTime's Group feature to engage in video calls with multiple participants simultaneously.

The Phone app serves as your gateway for voice calls, allowing you to easily make and receive calls. With features such as Call Waiting, Voicemail, and integration with your Contacts, the Phone app ensures seamless and reliable call management.

Beyond messaging and calling, the iPhone 15 also offers various other communication apps to meet your specific needs. Apps like WhatsApp, Skype, or Slack allow you to connect with colleagues, friends, or larger communities through messaging, voice, or video calls. These apps ensure that you stay connected and engaged with the people who matter most to you.

Furthermore, the iPhone 15 integrates seamlessly with other popular messaging services, ensuring that you can consolidate all your communication channels in one place. Whether it's iMessage, WhatsApp, Telegram, or others, you can receive and respond to messages from different platforms within the unified Messages app.

By leveraging the power of the Messages, FaceTime, Phone, and other communication apps on your iPhone 15, you can effortlessly stay connected, share moments, and foster meaningful relationships with your friends and family.

4.2 How to use Safari, News, Podcasts, Books, and other apps to browse the web and consume content

The iPhone 15 comes pre-loaded with several apps that cater to different content consumption preferences.

One of the most commonly used apps for web browsing on the iPhone 15 is Safari. Safari is a powerful and user-friendly web browser that allows you to access the internet and browse websites easily. With its intuitive interface and advanced features, Safari offers a seamless browsing experience on the iPhone 15.

Safari offers features like tabbed browsing, which allows you to have multiple websites open simultaneously in different tabs. This makes it easy to switch between different websites without losing your place. Safari also offers a reader view that removes distractions from web pages and presents the content in a clean, easy-to-read format.

Another app that facilitates content consumption on the iPhone 15 is News. The News app provides you with a personalized feed of news articles and stories from a variety of sources. You can customize your news feed based on your choice and preference. The News app also supports offline reading, allowing you to save articles to read later even when you are not connected to the internet.

If you enjoy listening to podcasts, the iPhone 15 comes with the Podcasts app. This app allows you to discover, subscribe to, and listen to your favorite podcasts. You can search for podcasts by topic, browse through popular podcasts, and create your own playlists to organize your podcast listening experience. The Podcasts app also supports automatic downloading of new episodes, ensuring that you always have fresh content to listen to.

If you're a book lover, you will find the Books app on the iPhone 15 to be a valuable tool for reading. The Books app allows you to browse and download a wide range of books, including bestsellers, classics, and even free titles. You can customize your reading experience by adjusting the font size, brightness, and background color. The Books app also offers features like bookmarks, highlights, and notes, making it easy to keep track of important passages or make personal annotations while reading.

In addition to these apps, the iPhone 15 also provides access to other content consumption services like Apple Music, Apple TV+, and the App Store. Apple Music is a music streaming service that offers access to millions of songs, curated playlists, and personalized recommendations.

Apple TV+ is a streaming service that offers a wide range of original TV shows, movies, and documentaries. The App Store is the official marketplace for iPhone apps, where you can download and enjoy games, productivity tools, social media apps, and much more.

Overall, the iPhone 15 offers a rich ecosystem of apps and services that cater to different content consumption needs. Whether it's browsing the web, reading books, listening to podcasts, or enjoying music, movies, and games, the iPhone 15 provides a seamless and enjoyable experience for you to stay entertained and informed.

4.3 How to use App Store, Apple Arcade, Apple Music, Apple TV+, and other services to download and enjoy games, music, movies, shows, and more

The App Store

The App Store is the primary platform for downloading apps and games on your iPhone 15. It offers a vast selection of apps and games, both free and paid, that cater to various interests and hobbies. You can search for specific apps or browse through categories to discover new ones. The App Store also provides user reviews and ratings to help you make informed decisions about the apps you want to download.

To make use of the App Store, tap on the App Store icon on your iphone home screen. From there, you can explore the featured apps, top charts, categories, and search for specific apps. When you find any app you want to download, click on it to view more details. You can then read the app description, check the screenshots and ratings, and even preview some apps before downloading them.

Apple Arcade
Apple Arcade is a subscription service that offers unlimited access to a curated collection of premium games. With Apple Arcade, you can enjoy a wide variety of games across different genres, all without ads or in-app purchases. The service is available to all users for a monthly fee and can be accessed directly from the App Store.

To subscribe to Apple Arcade, go to the App Store, tap on the Arcade tab at the bottom of the screen, and follow the prompts to sign up. Once you've subscribed, you can browse and play games from the Apple Arcade library. The games can be downloaded and played offline, making it convenient for long commutes or trips without an internet connection.

Apple Music
Apple Music is a popular music streaming service that offers a vast catalog of songs, albums, playlists, and radio stations. With Apple Music, you

can listen to your favorite songs and discover new music based on your preferences. The service also lets you create custom playlists, download music for offline listening, and access exclusive content from your favorite artists.

To start using Apple Music, open the Music app on your iPhone 15. If you already have an Apple Music subscription, sign in with your Apple ID to access your library. If you don't have a subscription, you can still sign up for a free trial and pay later in the app. Once you're signed in, you can search for songs, albums, artists, or playlists, and start streaming your favorite music.

Apple TV+
Apple TV+ is a subscription-based streaming service that offers original TV shows, movies, and documentaries created by Apple. With Apple TV+, you can enjoy high-quality content produced by renowned directors, actors, and writers. The service is available on your iPhone 15, Apple TV, and other Apple devices.

To access Apple TV+, open the Apple TV app on your iPhone 15. If you're already subscribed to the service, sign in with your Apple ID to start streaming content. If you're not subscribed, you can sign up for a free trial or subscribe directly from the app. Once you're signed in, you can browse through the available shows and movies, view trailers and previews, and start watching your favorite content.

4.4 How to use Health, Fitness, Wallet, Maps, and other apps to track your health, fitness, finances, travel, and more

The iPhone 15 comes with a range of built-in apps that can help you manage and track various aspects of your life. In this section, we will explore how to utilize the Health app, Fitness app, Wallet app, Maps app, and other related applications to keep track of your well-being, finances, travel plans, and more.

Health App:

The Health app is an all-in-one solution for managing and tracking your health and fitness data. It can monitor various aspects of your well-being, such as your heart rate, sleep patterns, steps taken, calories burned, and much more. You can also connect compatible fitness trackers or devices to the Health app to collect additional data. To get started, simply open the Health app and explore the available options to organize and view your health information.

Fitness App:

The Fitness app is designed to help you achieve your fitness goals. It offers a range of guided workout routines, personalized recommendations, and progress tracking features. Whether you want to build strength, improve endurance, or lose weight, the Fitness app can provide you with tailored workouts to suit your needs. Additionally, it can integrate with the Health app to collect comprehensive health and fitness data.

Wallet App:
The Wallet app is your digital wallet, allowing you to store and access various payment methods, such as credit and debit cards, loyalty cards, boarding passes, tickets, and more. With the Wallet app, you can make secure payments using Apple Pay, eliminating the need to carry multiple physical cards. You can also manage your Apple Cash balance, which allows you to send and receive money with family and friends.

Maps App:
The Maps app has been enhanced in the iPhone 15 to provide even more comprehensive and detailed navigation and travel information. You can use the Maps app to receive turn-by-turn directions, explore points of interest, find nearby places, and discover real-time transit information. Additionally, the Maps app integrates with other apps and services, such as ride-sharing apps, to provide seamless travel experiences.

Other Apps:
In addition to the above-mentioned apps, the iPhone 15 offers a wide range of other applications

that can help you track various aspects of your life. For example, the Stocks app can keep you updated on the financial markets, the Weather app can provide detailed forecasts, and the News app can deliver personalized news articles. Furthermore, the iPhone 15 supports a multitude of third-party apps that can further enhance the tracking and management of your health, fitness, finances, and travel.

By effectively utilizing the Health, Fitness, Wallet, Maps, and other apps on your iPhone 15, you can easily stay on top of your health and fitness goals, manage your finances, navigate to your destinations, and access a wealth of information and content. Take advantage of the powerful capabilities of these apps and discover new ways to enhance your daily life with your iPhone 15.

Chapter 5: Optimizing the performance and security of your iPhone 15

5.1 How to use Settings, Control Center, Notification Center, and other tools to customize your iPhone 15 experience

Settings:
The Settings app is like the control center of your iPhone. Here, you can personalize a range of options such as changing your wallpaper, adjusting display settings, configuring privacy and security settings, managing notifications, customizing Siri, and much more. It's a one-stop-shop for tailoring your iPhone experience.

Control Center:
Control Center gives you quick access to essential features and settings. To access it, swipe down from the top-right corner of your screen. In Control Center, you can enable or disable Wi-Fi, Bluetooth, Airplane Mode, and other settings, control media playback, adjust volume and brightness, activate the flashlight, and access shortcuts to apps and functions you use frequently. You can even customize the Control Center to include the features you often need.

Notification Center:
Notification Center keeps you updated with alerts and notifications. Swiping down from the top of the screen reveals your notifications, allowing you to view and interact with them quickly. You can customize which apps and alerts appear in the Notification Center, set priority levels, and choose how notifications are displayed.

Siri:
Siri is your virtual assistant, ready to help you navigate your iPhone and perform various tasks using voice commands. By customizing Siri settings, you can optimize its functionality, personalize its voice, and even create shortcuts for specific tasks.

These tools and settings allow you to tailor your iPhone experience to suit your preferences, making it more efficient, intuitive, and enjoyable. Customizing your device can enhance productivity and streamline everyday tasks.

5.2 How to use Battery Health Management, Low Power Mode, Fast Charging, MagSafe accessories, and other features to extend your battery life

Battery Health Management:
Battery Health Management is an intelligent feature that helps optimize the battery charging behavior of

your iPhone. It uses advanced algorithms to analyze your usage patterns and reduce battery aging. This feature can slow down battery aging and extend its overall lifespan.

Low Power Mode:
Low Power Mode is a convenient setting that conserves battery life by reducing power consumption. When activated, it adjusts various settings to minimize background activity, fetch new data less frequently, and dim the display. Low Power Mode helps your iPhone last longer when you're running low on battery.

Fast Charging and MagSafe accessories:
iPhone 15 supports fast charging, allowing you to charge your device quickly when you need a boost. Additionally, with MagSafe accessories, your iPhone can benefit from secure and efficient wireless charging. These features ensure you can power up your device rapidly and conveniently, reducing downtime.

By utilizing these features and implementing power-saving practices, you can extend the battery life of your iPhone 15, ensuring it remains functional and responsive throughout the day.

5.3 How to use Screen Time, Privacy, Security, Find My, Backup, and other features to protect your data and device

Here are some notable features that will help you to protect your data and maintain the security of your device:

Screen Time:
Screen Time empowers you to manage and monitor your device usage and app behavior. It provides insights into your daily screen time, app usage, and even allows you to set app limits, create downtime schedules, and establish content restrictions. With Screen Time, you can maintain a healthier balance between your digital life and real-world activities.

Privacy and Security settings:
Your iPhone 15 offers a range of privacy and security settings to protect your personal information. You can manage app permissions, control location services, fine-tune ad tracking settings, and enable features like Face ID or Touch ID for secure device access. Taking advantage of these settings and understanding their implications helps you keep your data private and secure.

Find My:
With the Find My feature, you can locate your iPhone if it's lost or stolen. This feature uses a combination of GPS, Wi-Fi, and cellular data to

track your device's location. It also enables remote actions such as playing a sound, activating Lost Mode, or remotely erasing your device to protect your data.

Backup options:
To ensure your precious data is safe and easily recoverable, iPhone 15 provides backup options that automatically back up your device to iCloud or your computer via iTunes. Regular backups can save you from the potential loss of important files, photos, contacts, and more. It's a simple and effective way to protect your data.

Conclusion: What's next for the iPhone 15 and Apple

As I conclude our journey through this user guide for the iPhone 15, it's worth contemplating what the future holds for this remarkable device and the innovative company behind it, Apple. While we can't predict every detail of what's to come, we can certainly discuss some possibilities and trends that might shape the future.

1. Technological Advancements: Apple has consistently pushed the boundaries of technology with each new iPhone release. We can anticipate continued advancements in processing power, camera capabilities, display technology, battery efficiency, and other hardware components. With each iteration, Apple strives to provide users with a more seamless, immersive, and intuitive experience.

2. 5G and Connectivity: The iPhone 15 already supports 5G connectivity, enabling faster download and upload speeds, reduced latency, and improved network reliability. As 5G networks expand and evolve, we can expect further integration of this technology into future iPhone models, enhancing the overall performance and connectivity options.

3. Augmented Reality (AR) and Mixed Reality (MR): Apple has been investing in augmented reality technology with features like ARKit and the LiDAR scanner. We may see further developments in this area, with more sophisticated AR capabilities that enhance gaming, productivity, education, and entertainment experiences. Additionally, there have been rumors and speculation regarding Apple's exploration of mixed reality, combining virtual and augmented reality. This opens the door to exciting possibilities for the iPhone's future.

4. Enhanced Privacy and Security: Privacy and security have always been priorities for Apple, and we can expect them to remain at the forefront in future iterations. The company may introduce additional features and improvements to protect user data, strengthen device security, and enhance user control over their personal information.

5. Environmental Sustainability: Apple has made significant efforts to reduce its environmental impact in recent years. We'll likely witness a continued commitment to sustainability, with more renewable energy initiatives, reduced packaging, increased use of recycled materials, and improvements in device recycling programs. Apple's dedication to environmental responsibility will likely be reflected in future iPhone models.

6. Software Updates and Integrations: Apple is well-known for its ecosystem of devices and services. We can anticipate further integration and synergy between the iPhone and other Apple products, allowing for seamless connectivity, data sharing, and synchronization. Additionally, Apple's software updates will continue to bring new features and improvements, enhancing the overall user experience.

It's important to note that these possibilities are based on trends and speculation and may not reflect every aspect of Apple's future plans. Apple is known for its commitment to innovation, surprise announcements, and adapting to changing consumer needs.

As we look ahead, what's next for the iPhone 15 and Apple is undoubtedly a journey of continuous improvement, cutting-edge technologies, and exciting new features. The iPhone has become an integral part of our lives, and Apple's commitment to delivering extraordinary user experiences makes the future of the iPhone and the company itself highly anticipated.